Women, Get Out of the Box!
You Are Called to the Ministry.

Rev. Katherine Schmidtke

XULON
PRESS

Xulon Press
11350 Random Hills Road
Suite 800
Fairfax, VA 22030
(703) 279-6511
XulonPress.com

To order additional copies, call 1-866-909-BOOK (2665).

Contents

PREFACE

A program on 'Larry King Live' was one of the reasons I was prompted to write the story of 'Women! Get Out of the Box. You Are Called to the Ministry". The program's purpose was to discuss the controversial by-law changes of the Southern Baptists, concerning the addition of the phrase "wives will graciously submit to their husbands."

The participants that made comments about this subject were Rev. Mohler (Baptist Theological Seminary), Rev. Jerry Falwell (Liberty University—Southern Baptist), Rev. Robert Schuller (Crystal Cathedral) and Pat Ireland (NOW representative).

The scripture being referred to, but never read, was Ephesians 5:22 "Wives, submit yourselves unto your own husbands, as unto the Lord." (NIV)

Rev. Schuller just couldn't relate to that scripture and

pointed out that he personally would never use the scripture in his sermons. He was more for 2 Corinthians 3:6b "not of the letter, but of the spirit: for the letter killeth, but the spirit giveth life." (KJV) Indicating that the word 'submit' is not a happy word. He recommends that a 60/40 relationship works best. Man as boss leads to head lock, 50/50 leads to dead lock, 60/40 leads to interlock. The interlock philosophy was unclear about who gets 60% and who gets 40%.

Rev. Jerry Falwell made his case that the headship of the husband was one of spiritual headship taking his family to church and making sure they were trained and taught the scriptures. He pointed out that his wife was smarter than he was and whenever they had a disagreement they did not proceed.

Pat Ireland of NOW was an interesting choice for the discussion of Biblical matters since she was not a Reverend, but she held her own in the discussion. Raising the point that the same book of Ephesians pointed out that slaves should submit to their masters. "Do you agree with that, Rev. Mohler?"

Rev. Mohler was adamant about the Souther Baptist's position in that the Bible is the inerrant word of God and wives are to submit graciously to their husband's leadership. And slaves (male or female) would be modeling what a good Christian is, when they submit to their masters, thus gaining the upper ground.

Somewhere along the line these learned folks missed the topic sentence which comes just before Ephesians 5:22 and that is 5:21 which states **"Submit to one another in fear of the Lord."** (KJV) **or "out of reverence for Christ"** (NIV). One another indicates that it is talking about more than one person and sure enough it is talking about wife and husband. In order to tie in the topic sentence with the next sentence the word "submit" is used and there it is, "Wives submit to your husbands." When the next person is talked about the word for submit is love. Ephesians 5:25 "Husbands love your wives," The concluding sentence to the theme of husbands and wives is found in Ephesians 5:33 "However, each one of you also must love his wife as he loves himself, and the wife must respect her husband."

If husbands and wives can submit to one another in fear of the Lord, there is a whole different understanding of what submit, love and respect means. For 'wives to submit graciously to the servant leadership of their husbands' doesn't have to be made into a by-law when husbands and wives are to love or submit to each other already.

The second prompting to write this book came as a result of watching Sixty Minutes with Ann Graham Lotz relating her story of running into gender bias towards women in the ministry.

When she stood up to preach at a preacher's convention a group of men turned their backs on her. That experience took her into the Bible. Fortified with the word of God she came out with this statement, 'when people have a problem with women in the ministry they need to take it up with Jesus, because He is the one who has put us there.'

On the same program Pastor James Merritt, president of the Southern Baptist convention was asked if he would have Ann Graham Lotz preach from his pulpit. "No", he would not. "There are two places where men are to be in head leadership, one is in the home and the other is as senior pastor of a church." To that remark, Ann Lotz said, "that idea has been pasted down from generation to generation. I wish I could bring a little fresh air from the Bible into their thinking."

Both of these thoughts, men in head leadership of the home and men only as senior pastors, are not in the Bible and they are discussed in the book "10 Lies the Church Tells Women", by J. Lee Grady.

The scripture that I could not explain away and caused our church a lot of problems was written by Paul and found in 1 Timothy 2:12 "I never let women teach men or lord it over them. Let them be silent in your church meetings".(NIV) And the reason why they were to keep quiet? Because they were not educated: they had no training. These were new believers who had come out of Gnosticism. In 1 Timothy 1:3-4 men were told to be silent because of their wild ideas. And in Titus 1:10-11 the believers were to stop 'these men' from speaking out with their lies.

That was then . This is now. Many women of today are educated in the Word of God just as some men are. God is selecting both men and women to serve Him in the ministry.

Because I know that God has called me into the ministry, I decided it was time to put the book entitled 'Women! Get Out of the Box. You Are Called to the Ministry' into circulation.

Chapter 1

BORN FOR A HIGHER PURPOSE

I was just an ordinary Christian believer, minding my own business, not interfering with anyone else about my beliefs, when my life was suddenly changed by an over night chance meeting with the Lord.

The sun was out on a beautiful summers day. Early in the morning, I suggested to my son that we visit a friend who lived on the lake. The house was nestled in the side of a hill about one hundred yards from a placid lake. As we walked into the colonial house, we were greeted by a clean smell and neat appearance.

As I visualize the scene now, I recall we had been visiting for about an hour and a half, enjoying a refreshing fruit drink, when we heard a commotion outside. Not only could we hear the sounds of sirens, but we could hear the muffled voices of people as they ran past the house. An electric charge filled the air.

We dashed to the door—opened it and ran outside. People were scurrying to a place by the edge of the lake. I knew that something was amiss. We inquired of a neighbor leaning out of her second story window if she could see what was happening. Quickly, she replied that it appeared someone had drowned.

It seemed now that our momentum moved in the same direction as all the other people. Heading toward the lake, I looked for my son, knowing that he would want to go with us. He wasn't to be seen, so I assumed that he was playing elsewhere and proceeded with my friend.

The rescue unit was there. We could see the men dashing back and forth getting the necessary equipment. The lights on top of the truck indicated—emergency! A look of fear and shock was in the eyes of all the people.

I remember leaving the side of my friend to get a closer look. I wanted to get through the crowd, but their arms and shoulders were pressed together so that I couldn't penetrate the circle. It seemed like hours went by. Everyone was intent on what was happening. A hush fell over the gathering. I heard the voice of an attendant say. "We've done all we can—have we done enough?" The crowd indicated that surely enough had been done! And then, I recall the man looking directly at me. His eyes locked onto mine. I heard myself saying, "Yes, yes, you've done enough." I could see that he was exhausted. His shirt was wet from perspiration. The others, too, looked drained from the exhaustion of the rescue operation.

The next sound I heard was the clanking together of the oxygen tanks—the men were moving out. It was finished. As the people turned to leave, I could see their faces. They seemed so plastic as they pasted me by as if I wasn't there.

I was alone. All alone with the sheet-covered body before me. I was curious to see who it was under the sheet. All the time thinking, it was too bad this had to happen, but that's life! It happens all the time. I bent down, pulled back the cover to reveal the lifeless face of my son!

Instantly, I knew that not enough had been done! "Oh, my God! My God! Help me." Tears came to my eyes. I fell to my knees. Beat on his chest—breathed into his mouth. Dear God, "Bring back my son from the dead. It can't be too late."

Then my thoughts raced back to the casual attitude I had had amongst the crowd. Why had I been so unconcerned? Why hadn't I become more involved? My whole being was caught up in a total feeling of anguish.

I awakened from this dream trembling. It shook me to the core. I needed to know what it meant. Not all dreams have a meaning, but I knew this one did. During the day it became clear.

To me, the rescue squad represented the hard-working preachers and evangelists who work so hard to spread the lifesaving gospel. The crowd of onlookers represented the Christians who are content to watch the clergy do the work. The dead body represented the non-Christians, those who do not have eternal life.

When I realized the dead body was that of my own son, I felt I had experienced the same feeling that Jesus feels for all people. It showed me that the same kind of love I have for my son, I must have for other people. You see, I wasn't personally concerned about the individual on that stretcher until I realized it was my own son—and then, not enough had been done!

If this dream taught me anything, it taught me that I must get involved—no longer can I sit in a church and do nothing. This experience happened to me in 1965, at a time when I was learning that Jesus was real and not just a "religion".

Chapter 2

A NEW DIRECTION

The direction and purpose of my life were different now. Three days later I got a call from my pastor asking me to get involved in a new program they were starting, "Evangelism Explosion". My first thought was 'no way'—what came out of my mouth, however, was let me check with my husband. I was learning to put God on the spot—'if you want me to do this, Lord, speak to me through my husband and I will know it is from you'.

With shaky legs I started the program. This program has two questions you ask a person followed up by a small simple brochure called 'Steps to Peace with God' that you could either hand to the person or go through it with them.

The very next day I was in a long line returning a Christmas gift only to find out I was in the wrong line. Praise the Lord any way. I must be missing a bad accident or something. Just as I finished the exchange and had turned to walk away a friend of my husbands took my arm and asked me to talk with him. He was in big trouble. He had walked out of the classroom after hitting one of his Special Ed students. What an opportunity, he was ready to respond to the two questions I had learned the night before. I actually didn't know where to go after the two questions until I reached into my coat pocket for a Kleenex and pulled out the brochure. It was so easy. He was ready to hear. It was the right spot, at the right time and I did it. It ended up being an appointment made in Heaven.

There was no end to the 'I want to do ministries' rather than 'the I should do it'. As a half day school teacher I started having lunch room Bible studies for any student who would like to brown bag their lunch with me. I became the teacher who could talk to big black bumble bees.

My room was on the sunny side of the school building— no air conditioning—so the windows were wide opened. A five minute recess for class passing gave a bumble bee the opportunity to buzz in. The kids were trying not to move, but their emotions took over, swotting, clinging to one another and running from one corner of the room to the other, so, I decided to pray, out loud. I just told the bee to go and to tell his buddies not to come back, in the name of Jesus. I asked the Lord to put up an invisible shield over the windows. When I was finished, the bee took an absolute directional turn to the window and flew out. From that time on I was known as the teacher who talks to bees. The lunch time Bible study was full all three lunches.

When I first started teaching in the public schools, the King James Bibles could be found in the discarded book room. This version was too difficult for my pupils. Once we were able to use the Living Paraphrased Bible the students were on their way to changed lives. In fact I was able to get enough Bibles for every student who took my class on Bible as Literature. A big problem developed when the other students wanted a Bible as well. Parents called the Principle's office and wanted to know why their kids couldn't have a Bible. This unfortunately caused a problem for me and I was transferred to another school the next year.

During the summer my two teenage sons would go with me to the parks where we set up a puppet stage and told stories from the Bible. It was not only successful for the kids in the parks but it was a wonderful learning experience for my boys and me. Building a stage out of PC pipe that was light and easy to put together, tape recording the different voices, making puppets for the Bible characters and writing the scripts each week made for an exciting summer, but also a training ground on making the Bible come alive.

As a family we started attending Faith Assembly Life Center. My husband with his Baptist background and, I, with a Lutheran—Presbyterian background found the freedom to worship and praise the Lord to our liking. After attending an altar workers class, Pastor Joe asked me if I would teach his class. Over a time span of twelve years the class expanded to three basic classes, Doctrines of the Holy Spirit, Evangelism/Counselor Training, and Signs Wonders, and Miracles. These classes developed believers to do the work of the ministry. Our healing teams had tremendous miracle stories to tell; eyes were healed, cancerous growths disappeared, a 70-yr old woman paralyzed on one side of her body got up out of her wheelchair in perfect condition. It was not difficult to get people to do the work of the ministry once they were equipped and knew how to work with the Holy Spirit. There were more than two hundred Care Group Leaders, our Evangelism Outreach Teams grew to thirty-eight, twenty-three Healing Teams, Altar Workers, 24 Hour Phone Counselors, Visitation Teams and Wednesday night call back teams incorporated hundreds of trained volunteers. It did not happen all at once, however.

In 1980, just shortly after my husband died of Lue Gehrig's disease, I started up a ministry called "THE LION OF JUDAH". It bothered me terribly that people were not reading their Bible even though they had several in their homes. A class comparing Bible translations convinced me that people liked and could understand the Living Paraphrased. My bed room became my sound proof room for the reading of the New Testament. It took three hours to record a twenty-eight minute segment. I had to contend with my hot water heating system when it started to click click click as the hot water expanded the pipes, and the south bound train whistle that went off around nine o'clock as it traveled along the Narrows. Going over and over the scriptures helped me out tremendously. It took about six months to complete the task of twenty-two tapes. Jimmy Swaggart

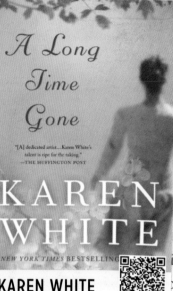

o use one of his music tapes which was
l to the voice. Once it was set to go
le 1981 the Year of the Bible and I was
en word out over the air ways without
st Radio picked it up several years later
e world.

ne that more people watch TV and
o have scenic pictures of the northwest
ing of the Bible. If someone else was to
uld cost two thousand dollars for each
ip to forty four-thousand dollars. As I
st of owning my own equipment and
doing my own selections for scenery I decided to buy the
equipment. What a risky thing that was. I was told that it
would take at least three years to learn how to use the equipment. Capital Communications agreed to give me eight
hours, two men for four hours. My oldest son came over and
he learned how to use and place the cameras and lights and
I learned how to use the mixing board and editing console.

I had a portable one inch recorder and camera and off I
went to take pictures. This was absolutely thrilling, chal-
lenging and frustrating at the same time. The camera, I
learned later had a miracle attached to it. The cord that went
to the camera and recorder was not made on this earth. The
connections on both ends were not compatible to the
recorder. I found this out when I tried to order another one
from the same company that sent it with the recorder. I could
have used a longer cord because sometimes I stretched the

cord and it would put a glitch on the tape. They told me they never sent a cord nor could they make a cord for my arrangement—totally impossible.

Once I got the Bible on video tape my son, who graduated from Oral Roberts University and was hired by a cable company, opened up the door to get the tapes on the air. The tapes were played up and down the West Coast.

I was not finished. I sat down at the table one evening and wrote down the next phase of the ministry. Three different types of programs were born THE KINGDOM OF GOD IS AT HAND dealing with personal testimonies of how Jesus changed their life. Seventy-nine programs came out of that program. Eighteen RESCUE documentaries were made having to do with the problems of our society and how to overcome them or minister to people caught up or addicted by them. WORLD IMPACT started with the statement 'What is Jesus doing in our world today?' Eighty-five tapes came from that series.

We looked like a four camera operation but had only two. An extra bedroom was used for operations with a wonderful volunteer manning the mixing board and the setting taking place in the living room of my home. I hosted, preached, moved cameras, set up lighting and did editing of the final production. The tapes were played over TBN Seattle and I was told they were the first Christian programs produced in our area. A span of seven years encompassed the radio and TV ministry and they were seen in many parts of the world.

The teaching atmosphere at school was changing and my

job security was becoming shaky.

Some of the students were watching the Lion of Judah programs and were asking me questions about the Lord. I felt free to respond but some other students reported my comments to the principal. I, of course, used every opportunity to share the Gospel with the principal or vice principal depending on whomever I had to respond to. I suppose the last straw for me came when an announcement came over the intercom about the teachers being able to wear Halloween costumes the next day. One of the student's comments to me was 'I suppose you don't give out candy'. **"Oh, yes I do, along with a Christian tract."**

That did it. The next day I got a registered letter requesting my presence before the principal; the divorced parents would be there, the student who made the complaint, the district office representative would be there, and I could have a Teacher's Union agent presence (taking place eight days from the day the notice arrived). After nineteen years it was time to join the union. Once the meeting took place and the story was out; the parents apologized, the district office shook my hand, the principle told me the student was out of line and added that I should not treat the student any differently in class and the union representative was very supportive.

Chapter 3

MEETING AN ANGEL

The strain of putting TV tapes together, teaching at public school (which was my only source of income) and teaching adult classes at Faith Assembly brought me to a place of crying out to the Lord over this matter. Returning home from a Sunday night's service, I started to sing and pray in my prayer language. When I finished, out of my mouth came 'ask pastor for a job'. This was not even in my thinking.

What kind of a job would I ask for?— In house evangelist.— That was it. I could hardly wait until Tuesday rolled around. As soon as I got into the office, 'I want you to hire me as your in house evangelist'.

Pastor's comment, "Perhaps you're the one I prayed for. Coming back from Korea on the airplane, I prayed for someone to head up our CARE group ministry."

Before my decision came to actually make this move, I

discovered I had some physical problems that doctors were investigating. I could sit and walk but I could not stand without feeling I would fall over and, as a matter of fact, I fell over at a Parent Teacher's night at school. There were sections all the way down my left side that were numb—a possible brain tumor. A brain scan revealed no problem. All sorts of tests were taking place. In the meantime I was to rest. I took a chance on a new chiropractor and he discovered my spine was out of alignment and that was more than likely what was causing the problem. The prognosis was that it usually takes about seven years to get full feeling back. Now the dilemma came. Should I leave my teaching job where there was health insurance that would cover anything that might end up being major or should I take the job at church which would not be so tense.

A chance meeting with what I felt was an angel gave me the answer I needed to make my decision. It was close to Christmas and something I was doing required some Elmer's glue. I went to the closet to bring out a newly purchased glue container only to find out, it was like stone. Payless drug store was near.

As I went to the isle where the glue was located, an older man was leaning over the display. Turning his face to look at me, he said, 'is this what you're looking for?' The conversation continued having to do with how he was going to use the glue. I continued on my way when he called to me. In his cart laid a shopping bag black with gold trim—very unusual covering. Inside were two different colored star shapes that he wanted to glue together. As I turned to go, the thought came to me, I need to tell him about Jesus. He was gone. Where did he go? I looked up the other isles but he was no where insight. This chance meeting did not leave me. When the impression came to me at home that I had seen an angel, the phone rang with a call from a friend who had a message to tell me. A lady she had visited in the hospital that very day had an encounter with an angel who told her to read Exodus 23:20-26. Eunice, not knowing the circumstances in my life, felt it was a message for me.

Ex. 23:20 "See, I am sending an Angel before you to lead you safely to the land I have prepared for you....23 for my Angel shall go before you and bring you into the land ...." This was a good word. Sunday morning I read it again and the nagging problem of health was answered when I read verses 25—26b, "You shall serve the Lord your God only; then I will bless you with food and with water, and I will take away sickness from among you. 26b, and you will live out the full quota of the days of your life." (TLB) I had my directions.

Chapter 4

A NEW BEGINNING

January 1987 I became a staff member at Faith Assembly as the Director of Evangelism and Small Group Ministries. The actual responsibility was not difficult because I was already doing the ministry at the church but was now director and getting paid. My healing came gradually and didn't interfere with the ministry for I was doing the work that God had trained me to do. For the last twelve years I had the privilege of training people to be CARE Group leaders without knowing that is what they would be doing. When the call went out for leaders and assistant leaders, there they were, eighty-three faithful workers ministering to more than 400 people monthly. Two new classes became available for the visitor, inquirer and new Christian called "Discovery" and "Fresh Start". Sometimes people who come to a large church get the idea that there are clicks and that they don't feel like they fit in, and that may be true. So, how do you work with that idea in a positive way because groups are not bad. The Discovery class met that need as they met with other new people for four weeks with a husband and wife team for round table discussions.

The new folks all had something in common with each other; they were new and wanted to know more about what Faith Assembly was all about and how did Faith Assembly's beliefs match up with theirs. Our leaders were able to answer their questions biblically and misconstrued ideas were put to rest. The leader along with the new attenders continued the round table fellowship in another room with six other round tables containing new folks as old as six months, five months, four months and so on.

Fresh Start went on for six months, giving the new folks an opportunity to fit in. Seven months later they were in a CARE group with the same leader they had in the beginning. We encouraged these folks to come on Wednesday night and take the Growth Classes that would train them for leadership. This was one successful program, but for me, it was about to change.

Chapter 5

BURNING BUSH EXPERIENCE

I t all started with what I would call a burning bush experience. I was in England at the Rienhart Bonnke convention on July 22, 1988. It was 3:00 a.m. in the morning. I thought at first I must have been sick, or the room had over heated, but it was none of those things. This went on for about an hour until out of my mouth, without even thinking, came these words, "Lord, is this you?" Immediately a conversation took place. I didn't see Him, but I knew He was there and it all seemed so normal.

Like a scroll being unrolled He showed me a plot of land in Tacoma, Washington. It zoomed in so I could see exactly what piece of property was being focused on, even to the name of the streets. A clear directive came to me. "You are to build a church, high school and center. The church will have a 3,000 seat capacity and will be filled twice on a

Sunday morning. The school will hold 750 students." The center was not elaborated on at that time.

A conversation ensued with questions from me and answers from the Lord. Questions like "How is this to be built?"—"YOU DON'T HAVE TO WORRY ABOUT THAT, I WILL DRAW THE PEOPLE." "Where will the money come from?"—"YOU DON'T HAVE TO WORRY ABOUT THE FINANCES: I WILL SUPPLY THEM." "Who will pastor the church?"—"YOU ARE TO PASTOR THE CHURCH." "Why would you select a woman?"—"I HAVE NOT SELECTED A WOMAN. I HAVE SELECTED A VESSEL."

Much conversation later, for this took about an hour, I fell asleep thinking it would all be forgotten in the morning. Not to be the case, however, for when I woke up it was on my mind to write and diagram out what had transpired and what had been said.

The speaker the next morning was Jack Hayford from California. His main conversation centered around "If God has given you a dream or a vision during this convention, write it down." Then he proceeded to talk about what God had done in his church as a result of a dream that the Lord gave him about a plot of land for future church growth.

On returning home, I did nothing about this experience, thinking it would go away and half hoping it would go away. And yet, I was absolutely excited about having had this experience with the Lord. Believe me, when God talks to you, you know it! But because of its immensity, I thought possibly a mistake had been made. So I was looking for more bench marks, or pieces of the puzzle to fit together before I went off the deep end. I had not the slightest idea of what to do first, or how to proceed. I went by the property just to see if it was truly there and would make Saturday passes to claim it for the Lord. In January I found out who owned the property.

Getting a map from the city planning department, I discovered the land was owned by the husband of a friend from my college days. When I gathered up courage to talk to the owner, I fully expected him to reject my idea. I laid it out just as the Lord had given me the experience. The owner confessed that they were in the process of dividing the land for sale, but it would take a little time so I didn't have to rush. When I heard this, I could hardly believe my ears. He wanted to know how much property we needed for the project. In fact he drove me all over showing me what he owned.

I had no idea how much of the property we would need to build the project so I contacted a builder who delayed a week before he could view the property.

During that period of time an unusual coincidence took place. A piece of paper fell out of a Bible I seldom used revealing a dream I had written down on August 13, 1986, two years earlier. The significance of this sheet of paper became very important to my getting more involved in this venture. For the dream was about a 'pair of boots' that I was to get or buy and the value of fifteen million dollars was stated by a person who was on top of the roof who could see the whole thing.

When the builder came to look at the land, I asked him what he thought the project would cost. His report was twelve to fifteen million dollars, the same figure that was stated on the sheet of paper that was written down two years earlier. He also commented it would be a perfect place to build a church, high school and center because of the road access and location of the property. Again, instead of a closed door the door swung wide opened.

The coincidence of the two-year-old dream came into play again. The dilemma of just exactly how much property was needed was solved when I spoke to the owner weeks later. He told me to get three maps of the land from a survey company that had worked on the land several years before. When I went to pick up the maps I noticed with great amazement that a see-through transparency had outline marks on it and in one section, showing up as plain as day, was a 'pair of boots'. A female heel and a male heel somewhat overlapping one another. Now we knew exactly what portion of the property we were to pray for.

Why had I saved that dream or even written it down? Why did it fall out at this time? Why did I go to that particular Bible to find an unrelated answer? All of those questions were important to my going on with this project.

Chapter 6

LEAVING IS
NOT SO EASY

L eaving Faith Assembly was not on my mind as I enjoyed the responsibility, position and security I had at church as the Director of Evangelism. I anticipated continuing on there but the idea of doing something about this experience was constantly on my mind even though I tried to push it out of the way. I somehow hoped that the church would be built and I would then be called to pastor it. That seemed easy to me. But easy was not what was called for.

I shared a portion of my experience with my pastor in hopes that he would say I was out of order. But he thought I could build a church and pastor it. He recommended I get twelve families and go. Once I had shared with him, he continued to remind me as the months slipped by that the window of opportunity only lasts so long and I was not getting any younger. I felt pushed when I didn't want to go into the unknown.

I can honestly say that things were pretty tense for a while. The battle to go into the unknown seemed like earthquake conditions, and the push from my pastor to go, turned what I thought solid ground into sinking sand. My mind was spinning around for what God really wanted me to do.

Three incidences, taking place in a 24-hour period of time, put me over the edge to realize I must go. I wanted to put my mind at rest so I watched a video. During a most precarious time in Israel's history Goldia Meyer was in New York to solicit funds for the war that was sure to come. One of the last lines she gave to the people was, "If not now, when?" From out of no where these words hit my heart like a bomb. I quickly turned the video off and went to bed. I couldn't believe God would disturb me when I was trying to rest from the confusion that was going on in my head.

Sleep was slow to come that night. Around 3:00 a.m. I woke up. Immediately I turned on T.V. hoping that would lull me to sleep again. First thing on T.V. came these words from a man who thrust his fist out, "Do it now." Again these words hit home. Whoever heard of a woman pastor? Surely this wasn't God's will. The next night, I watched a T.V. documentary of the Korean war. Surely I would have peace tonight. McArthur was speaking these words. "If not now, when? If not you, who?" That did it. If not you, who? Had God asked others who refused? Was there something in me that He wanted to use? These questions haunted me until the next day when I responded to the call of God on my life. Sink or swim I must do it.

It was agreed that I would leave my position at Faith Assembly at the end of the month. The Sunday before I was to depart there was a note on my door to meet with pastor on Monday. It was in my thinking that he wanted to give me some helpful advise. Normally Monday was our day off. As I walked into the room I was faced with five other pastors, three from church, one from district office and one from another church. It became obvious to me that this meeting had started before I arrived. I was immediately bombarded with incriminating statements like, I had not followed procedures to start a new church, the neighborhood pastors were not informed, District office was not aware. A lamb to the slaughter has real meaning to me now. My heart was pounding like mad and I wanted to leave several times. My own pastor whom I had told seven to eight months earlier said he had not been informed. His advice at the time was to take twelve couples and go—the window of opportunity only lasts so long and at another time "when are you going, you are not getting any younger". The Northwest district person sat quietly knowing I had informed the district and had gotten direction as to the proper procedure to follow, the neighborhood pastor and I had met in his office earlier and talked about the starting of the church and ended our meeting with a prayer. This had all been forgotten apparently and I was left with I can't believe this is happening. I did learn a valuable lessen from this meeting, however: Never go alone, know what the agenda will be, take a tape recorder if possible and take notes after the meeting.

Chapter 7
STEPPING OUT

August 6, 1989 was my last Sunday at Faith Assembly. It came fast once the decision was made. I told the Lord that it would not be good for me to have my office at home. One week before I was to leave, a call came from a family that had an office in a complex not far from the land, offering me free office space. I was delighted when I arrived to find a lovely spot to hang my coat. Above the office was a large board room where we held our first meetings. About twenty people showed up including a Filipino man and his family who led us in worship with his sardivarious. (Strings attached to a sardine can and stick.)

A larger complex right next door was miraculously made available to us to use with an upstairs, many rooms for Sunday school classes, and a large foyer as well as a nursery room and three restrooms. Donated desks from a relocating company were exchanged for 120 chairs. An organ and piano were donated. Song books came from a garage sale as we canvassed the neighborhood with the Gospel. God truly blessed us as we started walking the path He laid before us.

The month, before we opened our church, was filled with preparation, miracles and frustrations. I learned how to use the computer, a wonderful experience when you have someone at your beckon call to correct your mistakes but most frustrating when you lose all sorts of information by pushing the wrong button. One of the remarkable works of God was the way he spoke to people who knew nothing about what we were doing who came along side because God had spoken to them to get involved. Pizza Answer owners opened their space for our first few meetings just as we were outgrowing the upper room, a strip mall owner opened up a former dentist's office— rent free for six months. Next move was to a larger room formerly used as a pet store. My oldest son put wall partitions, built a stage, an office, nursery and foyer. Helpers, wood and rug all came in without cost.

Now we were growing so a monthly cost of $400.00 a month was charged. The new AMVET building was opened up to us just as we had to vacate the pet store. We signed a year's lease for Sunday all day, Tuesday morning and Wednesday evening. We rented an office space not far from our previous location where we had to store our loud speaker system and equipment for Sunday sessions. A slight smell of beer and smoke was left over from the night before but they set up the chairs and kept it clean for us. On Pentecost Sunday the fire engines came thinking there was a fire. It fit right into the sermon that was preached that Sunday. They were glad to see us go at the end of our lease because they were able to rent the same space on Saturday night for fifteen hundred dollars.

Our next move was for three winter months in a building occupied by other businesses. The automatic heating system didn't kick in on Sunday morning—evening or Wednesday night because the other businesses worked on weekdays during the day. Our little kids really suffered and the adults wore heavy coats. Even though the thermostat had a warning not to touch, I touched and got into big trouble with the owner so we were asked to leave.

Just two blocks away was a small strip mall with two empty spaces that had never been rented. This was a wonderful spot right in the middle of apartment village. We were learning that this is where the schools of fish are located. The rooms had never been rugged so the first Sunday service the younger kids would sit in the chairs with one foot under the other leaving a chalk mark from their shoes which came from the chalk like substance from the floor. Simple little prayer "Oh, Lord, we can't have another Sunday like this. We must have rug." Monday morning, just before nine o'clock I stopped at a hardware store close to my home and there on the outside of the building were rolls of rug they were removing from their display sections going for five dollars apiece. I contacted the manager and asked if our church could have them. He said yes if we could get them out before noon. "Absolutely" Just as I turned to leave there was a former student of mine as a cashier. "Do you have a truck?" His answer was in the positive but it was a small truck and he couldn't leave until his lunch break. It was a done deal.   When I got to the location of our church, my older son walked in. **"What do you need Mom?"** "You can't believe it, but I can have the rug from the hardware store." It just so happens that Stan had called the storage company that was storing our chairs and desks to bring them over to our church. When he called them back they willingly dropped by the hardware store and picked up the rugs. When they dropped the rug off, they placed it around the room.

That afternoon a friend came over whose husband was a professional rug layer and he volunteered to lay the rug down. It covered both spaces except for a twelve by ten foot area and he had extra carpeting for that area. Sunday morning we had one hundred and twenty chairs prepared for our celebration. We had a few extra desks that were traded for room dividers that gave us a nursery room next to the office, two class rooms and the main sanctuary. A department store gave us material for swag curtains to cover the windows. Boy, did we look good. These two sections were valued at three thousand dollars a month. We rented them month by month for five hundred dollars. This we prayed would be our last move until we moved to "the pair of boots" property.

As we went out to knock on doors and let people know we were starting a new work in the Chambers Creek area we discovered, after 2,500 people responded, that our area had 60 to 70% Catholic families with 3 to 4 % attending church consistently; Unity, New Age came in at about 10%; Baptist, Lutheran, and Presbyterian 13%; Full Gospel 2% and those with no church back ground came in at 5%. Interesting things about the Catholics, they didn't go to church because they feel they had committed the unpardonable sin and therefore could not attend and they can't attend another type of church because they believe the Catholic church would not approve.

Our ministry centered around 75% of the people and we sent out a classy brochure about the dream and vision God had for their area. As an alumni of the University I found a friend in the print shop who worked miracles for us. Our brochures were made of many different colors, left over paper from university jobs. Our team of workers placed 7.000 brochures in newspaper boxes, tagged the doors and passed them out at the stores.

Chapter 8

A SPECIAL ANOINTING— AMAZING

An anointing that is for a specific calling or job is awesome. I can only speak of the anointing that was so different from anything I've ever experienced when we set out to do the assignment of building a church, high school and center. This was a special anointing that came for each task I was called to do. Ideas came quickly. Sermons were there—no struggle. The anointing possessed the delivery, came with prophecy, and convicted those who came. This particular anointing was nothing I could work up, but was definitely amazing. It was an anointing for the job to be accomplished. The need was the deed. When we had to move from one location to the next—there was direction immediately—no missed Sundays—no panic.

Jobs that had to be done were accomplished by others who were notified by the Holy Spirit. For example; my older son came at the right time to notify the movers to pick up the rug for our church, everything was synchronized, I was not involved except to say that the rug is over there. Another example: It cost us three hundred dollars to put on a Vacation Bible School that ended up not being cost effective for us because the children who came were attending other churches already and the parents used our program for baby-sitting. We were interested in getting those who didn't attend church. As the next summer was approaching, an idea came to me. Just as the idea came a young man walked in the door and told me that the Lord spoke to him in a dream and told him he would be mightily used in the new church just South of his home. I learned more about him and that he was a baker who got home from work about two thirty. Perfect. The idea required one person to play organized games with the kids who were coming home from school and being dropped off at their apartments around three. The apartment managers gave the O.K.. Kenton and I did this for a week on each campus—three o'clock to four and then invite them to Wednesday evening "Live Wire".

Fourteen apartment complexes in a three-block radius packed in a lot of people in a small space. The sound of gun fire and the buying and selling of drugs was familiar to the young kids that came to "Live Wire". Believing the message that Jesus was in their midst brought immediate salvations and a definite change in their lives. The testimony of Jesus appearing to two girls as they walked from their apartment to church and an eight-year-old boy seeing Jesus when he went to bed, brought his father and mother to church the next Sunday and encouraged others to come.

This program not only got us on apartment campuses but opened the door to other ministries. The 7-11 store manager was the first to tell us that the drug dealings on their corner disappeared after we came on the scene. Even the apartment managers recognized that drugs and gun shots were going down on their campuses. Some even gave us the green light to use their rec-rooms for adult programs. Because we visited the apartment people, we discovered their needs: unemployment, depression, crime, drugs, poverty, no mothering skills, poor education, broken families, anti social behavior and lack of trust.

Getting off of Welfare, The Joy of Working, Work a Budget, Marriage Enrichment, and How to Select a Mate were a few of the programs to the apartments. We never missed the opportunity to share the love of Jesus with each program that got us in the opened door. Twenty-three volunteers, one paid staff member and seven board members worked to bring a little light to a dark corner.

Chapter 9

FRIENDLY FIRE

St. John's Shipyard became world famous during the 2nd World War. My grandfather would take us to a hill overlooking the christening and we would watch the huge battle ships slide down the dry docks into the river. Interesting thing about that particular time in history; women and men worked side-by-side to get a job done. There was a war going on and everyone was needed.

Today there is a different kind of war going on—a fight for the souls of men, women, boys and girls. It seems rather odd to me that only men can fulfill the call of the ministry, especially when Jesus calls us all to fulfill his commission.

When we left Faith Assembly to start our new work in the Chambers Creek area, all hell broke loose. It seems I had violated the ethics procedure and had not received the blessings of the neighborhood pastors who just happened to be all men and believed that women were not to be in the role of a Pastor.

Several days before I received a letter from the District Office, I had a night dream that was a foretelling of the events that were about to take place in my life. Only after the horrendous experience took place did the dream make any sense to me. And then it was a great comfort to know that the Lord was in control of all circumstances.

"As I walked into the room I could see that the mantel over the fire place was filled to capacity with the pictures of important men. Another picture was squeezed into the group. Voices from the portraits became agitated over this person that was placed in their midst. I could only see the back of the robed, white-haired figure who placed the portrait on the mantel. The new picture was pushed to the floor by the other pictures. A voice of authority, that every portrait submitted to, proclaimed—'Make room for her ministry!' His voice shook my whole being. As I walked forward to look at the faces, I recognized a few of the men but the woman's face looked like mine." What did this dream mean? It was only after the following experiences took place did I reread the dream and realized that God knew in advance what I and our church were to go through.

Even to tell this story, I have had to question my motives as to whether this part of the battle needs to be told. Not telling the story in all of its Glory only gives a strong foothold to the spiritual principalities that must come down if the Gospel of the Kingdom of God is going to go out unhindered. The circumstances that took place as I entered into the clear-cut plan of God to build a church, high school and center in the Chambers Creek area, in my opinion, has actually revealed the principalities that are stifling the work of the Kingdom.

On August 31,1989, I received a letter from Brother Bosco, the Assistant Superintendent of the Northwest District of the Assembly of God, that prompted me to respond with the following letter dated September 2, 1989.

Dear Brother Bosco:

In response to your letter of August 31, 1989, I would like to set the record straight. In all that I have done I have followed the procedure that you and Pastor Bell recommended. Not knowing how to begin, I relied on men that I thought would give me knowledgeable advice. Pastor Wade was the first to recommend I talk with Pastor Bell and with the Northwest District.

On February 23, 1988, I told Pastor Bell about the fact that I had an experience with the Lord. I felt the Lord wanted me to build a church and I felt He wanted me to be the Pastor of that church. His response was positive in that he thought I could build a church and it was not impossible for me to pastor one. These two questions were uppermost in my mind as to what he thought on these two questions.

Several weeks later he asked me when I was going to get started. Let the record show that I was not interested in being pushed nor was I really anxious to get started. I was looking for more bench marks along the way. It was at this time he told me that twelve families would be needed to start. At that time, I did nothing but wait upon the Lord.

Again, several weeks later Pastor Bell came into my office wanting to know when I was going to get started. He proceeded to tell me that every opportunity has a window of time and then it is gone. He also mentioned that I was not getting any younger.

At his urging and believing that God could be speaking through Pastor, I then called and made an appointment with you to get direction as to how I was to proceed. You, Brother Bosco, canceled the appointment. I called to make another appointment and learned that you would be in Tacoma on Friday to work with House of Prayer. Not hearing from you on Thursday, I called House of Payer on Friday morning and we made an appointment to meet at Road Way Inn. Besides myself, Pastor Hill, Pastor Shoemaker and you, were present. The conversation centered around the planting of new churches for the Decade of Harvest—Lakewood, Dupont, Fircrest were mentioned—right in the center of Chambers Creek.

You and I went to another table where I shared with you along with showing you a map of the area God had shown me to plant a church. Not knowing what to do or how to proceed and believing you were responsible for giving me that information, I listened to you with acute detail. Your comments were that I was to get a board together and, that this would be a sovereign church rather than a missions church. You went into some detail about the difference: A sovereign church starts on its own and then when it is established it is brought into the fellowship, whereas, a missions church starts as a result of the fellowship planting a church in a location. I also shared that I felt a temporary structure was to go on the property to start with—tent like. You recommended that I visit Pastor Joe's Church of which I did the next day, Saturday. I asked you point-blank if I should share this further information with Pastor Bell and your response was not to.

On your information that you gave and Pastor Bell's, I proceeded to follow your directions and invited close friends (after twenty years at Faith Assembly this is where my close friends were) to an evening at my place to share with them all the information about my experience with the Lord and about the response I had from both Pastor Bell and you.

Pastor Bell continued to ask when I was going to move on with the new church. Either the last week in June or the first week in July, being under such pressure to share all with him, I sought Pastor Bob's advice as to whether I should tell Pastor Bell all of what was happening. He recommended I do just that and it was on this day that I shared with Pastor all, including the meeting I had with Brother Bosco and the fact that I was told not to share all with Pastor Bell.

It was at this meeting that Pastor Bell recommended that my last day be on July 30, 1989. I countered that August 30, be my last day. He countered with August 6th being my last Sunday with vacation to cover any fear of not having a salary for a month.

I would like the record to show also that Brother Bosco and I were to have had a meeting with Pastor Harris of a neighborhood Church, but because of your busy schedule you recommended that I speak to him on my own. This I did on August 11, 1989. At that meeting I shared the location of the property on 67th and Bridgeport Way West. He later said at a meeting with Pastor Bell, John, Brother Bosco, Pastor Harris and me on August 15, 1989 that I didn't give him a chance to respond and that he thought the church was to be much further away.

I would like to go on record and state that he knew exactly where the "gravel" pit was for he was the one that used that term. Furthermore, he knew that it was this side of the car dealership rather than on the other side because that was established at the meeting he and I had. He stated I gave him no opportunity to respond to what I had shared, but on the contrary I specifically asked, "do you see any problems that could arise out of planting a church there?", for this was the only purpose for the meeting.

Finally, I want the record to show that I have made every effort to do what I was lead to believe were direction and guidance from learned men. After following yours and Pastor Bell's directions, I have discovered that the guidance was faulty and I am now to believe that I have broken "fellowship" and that my credentials with the Northwest District of the Assemblies of God are in jeopardy. My question is, how could that be when I have followed your directions? It is my belief that the "brethren" have been a bit sloppy in their advice and guidance, but—and let the record show—that I don't wish to disassociate myself with the Assemblies of God.

Further more, let the record show, that after waiting one month (one month being the specified time that Pastor Bell said was required of me to be away from Faith Assembly—August 6th being my last Sunday) Chambers Creek Christian Center will start church September 10th—temporary location to be 4007 Suite D Bridgeport Way.

It is my prayer that there will be cordial fellowship and cooperation between all concerned and we can concentrate on winning the lost into the Kingdom of God.

Sincerely, Katherine E. Schmidtke."

I received a letter from the Northwest District, dated January 15, 1990, requesting my resignation from the fellowship or I would be dismissed. "The District Presbyters in session on October 4, 1989 passed a motion to begin the process to dismiss Katherine Schmidtke as a licensed minister with the Northwest District Council." My response was of surprise and shock. How could this happen? I felt I had followed all procedures requested of me. What had I done? Our church was basically one month old when this meeting took place.

The letter did have one option for me. I could request an appeal. I chose to appeal.

My response letter to the January 15th letter was rather crisp.

January 19, 1990

Dear Mr. Kelly,

I am absolutely shocked at the response the District Presbytery has taken concerning my license as a minister with the Assemblies of God. I take the stand that the decision you have taken, which started October 4, 1990, before I had an opportunity to air my side of the story, is unjust, unchristian, unwarranted, and very much out of order.

Let the record show that I have no intentions of turning in a resignation letter but on the contrary, I make this a letter of complaint against Pastor Bell; who advised me, after sharing with him my burning bush experience, to get twelve families together and go build the church; and against Brother Bosco, who was the first to advise me to get a board together and start. It was at this meeting that he advised me not to share the whole story with Pastor Bell because it was not necessary. Enclosed is a response letter from Brother Bosco proving that we did have a meeting. Because of following their advice I am now found guilty of following their advice and they are now saying it was wrong advice to take. Well, they have put me in a position of encouraging me to take parachute lessons, pushing me out the plane and on my way out the door one of them shouts, 'The rip cord is missing.' In my book, this is criminal activity and needs to be punished.

To insinuate that I have broken fellowship is ludicrous and uncalled for. On the contrary, I have gone out of my way to meet with Pastor Harris to discuss the location of Chambers Creek Christian Center (high school and church). Pastor Harris's Church is about as close to Faith Assembly as Chambers Creek Christian Center will be to Pastor Harris's Church. I have cooperated with Pastor Bell's restrictions as I left Faith Assembly to start the new work and have in no way acted unbecoming in my position as a licensed Assembly of God Pastor. Enclosed is the September 2 letter to Brother Bosco.

It is because of this that I will be accepting the right to a hearing with an impartial board.

Sincerely,

Katherine E. Schmidtke—Pastor/Evangelist"

I received a Certified letter dated January 25, 1990, signed by Mr. Kelly to attend a meeting on Tuesday, February 6, 1990 at the Northwest District office at Kirkland to meet with the committee at 10:30 a.m.

Five members from our church accompanied me to Kirkland where I was allowed to have my oldest son present with me in the presence of twenty-four District Presbyters and my accuser's Pastor Bell and Pastor Harris.

In brief, I had to respond to the two basic reasons for my being brought before the District Presbyters.

1. The soliciting of Faith Assembly people to come and help build the church.

   My response:

   A. Pastor Bell recommended I get twelve families and go. It was not my idea.

   B. The Northwest Messenger magazine lists this as a way to plant a church.

   C. Faith Assembly has started several churches with people from Faith Assembly. The book Joy of Belonging gives the details.

2. It is the policy to meet with Pastors affected by any new church location and obtain their opinion.

   My response:

   A. Refer to Brother Bosco's letter of April 21, 1989 which clearly deletes any reference to this fact.

B. Brother Bosco never recommended nor did he plan a meeting with the other pastors of Tacoma.

C. Northwest Messenger magazine October 1989 lists Fife, Dupont and Fircrest as places to plant a church. Our location is on the edge of Fircrest.

D. The two other pastors, Hill and Shoemaker recommended Lakewood, Dupont, Fircrest and Steilacoom as places to start churches at the meeting that took place some time in March. Our church location is in the middle of three of those named as possible places to plant a church.

E. The fact that this was a sovereign church not a missions church.

The twenty-four Presbyters were then given the opportunity to ask questions of both Pastor Bell and myself.

In concluding the hearing, I was given an opportunity to sum up my position.

1. Pastor Bell is responsible for telling me to get twelve families and go. And therefore I can't be found guilty of soliciting members from his church as a result of following his advice. And if I am found guilty, he is the instigator of the crime along with the Northwest Messenger magazine.

2. I was never informed or notified by brother Bosco that I was to get the pastors from Tacoma together to get input from them and therefore can't be found guilty on these grounds. And if I am found guilty—he is guilty of not informing me when I came for directions on what to do.

3. I was never given an opportunity to share with the pastors of Tacoma the plan, but instead have been threatened with expulsion because I didn't share with them. I can't be found guilty of something I didn't have an opportunity to do.

We were dismissed to wait in the foyer until the Presbyters came to their conclusion.

How did we get to this point? Why couldn't we be friendly people? Weren't we supposed to be working together to further the Kingdom of God? Why did the dream and vision have such a hornet's nest affect on Pastor Bell? For twenty years of my life I put my gifts of teaching adults, counseling at the altar, phone ministry, training and building the body of believers at Faith Assembly. And then, when the Lord calls me to do a work for him, why this reaction?

The twenty-four presbyters had made their decision and we were called back into the room. It was unanimous, the twenty-four presbyters felt that I had broken no breach of fellowship.

Did I feel happy about this conclusion? Absolutely, yes.

But still I wondered why did we have to get to this point? What was it in me that caused such a violent response from my Pastor? As we got up to leave, the district Superintendent who was sitting next to me shook my hand and at the same time asked the question, "Why do you think he did this to you?" My answer came out so unencumbered, "I am a woman." His response was, "I thought so." I was rather surprised that I would make that confession and I was even more surprised that he recognized the spiritual principality at work.

A follow-up letter dated March 16, 1990 stated that my credentials remained intact. It also stated that upon receiving and approving an application for Chambers Creek Christian Center to become affiliated with the Assemblies of God, the church would be received into fellowship. On June 21, 1990, our church's name became Chambers Creek Assembly of God and my Ordination papers came on April 22, 1991.

I don't include these letters to prove my case. No! No! No! I include these letters to show the work of principalities that are trying to derail the furthering of the Kingdom of God. I could understand the position that Pastor Bell took of wanting to protect his flock and his kingdom. But, I had to respond to the call of God. As difficult as it might seem, when the Lord spoke so dramatically in my life, I had to listen to His voice and respond.

Knowing that we do not wrestle against flesh and blood, but against spiritual principalities, I was shocked that they (the principalities) were able to use someone I had grown to love and respect throughout my twenty-three years at Faith Assembly.

Four years later, when I had an opportunity to talk about this experience with Pastor Bell, I asked him why he didn't help us. Without any hesitation on his part came these words; "Oh! I wouldn't help a woman pastor and neither would our church board." There it was—in all of its Glory.

Chapter 10

DID WE MAKE A DIFFERENCE?

When we started our church, September 10, 1989, we were full of excitement. With a bright future before us and the knowledge that this was God's idea, not man's: how could we fail?

Plans were made to have a city-wide Prayer Breakthrough. We wanted this new work to be covered in prayer. The hall was scheduled, the praise singers were assigned, the announcements and advertisements were released. News came from my former pastor that I was out of order and the Prayer Breakthrough was to be canceled. Not wanting to cause any trouble we canceled it.

O.K., it was decided that we would target our area of ministry with prayer. We would not interfere with the vineyards of the other churches. Because of that decision we were able to discover that crime and vandalism went down in our area and crime and vandalism went up in the areas all around our targeted area. Was that just coincidental?

On the wall we placed a map of the county. We prayed just strictly for our area. We drove around it, visited individual homes with a survey, learned about the people, introduced them to our new work, mailed our church brochure and just generally learned about our neighbors.

Every Sunday or Wednesday night we had praise, worship and action prayer, the kind of prayers that killed the giants. The giants were listed in the newspaper headlines, and we knew the problems of the area because we were getting to know the people. We were unaware of the effects of our prayer workout until sometime in the beginning of 1993, when we were getting rather desperate for money.

By this time we had moved six times. Most of the wonderful air-conditioned buildings that we occupied were for a short duration until the manager could get the full rental price for the space. All of the places we used were at a fraction of the cost of what it could be rented for.

Moving was hard on growing our church body because people like stability; they don't like change, and many didn't have transportation to the next location. So, when we got the manager's letter that we would have to pay the full price plus sign up for five years, I made a request for financial help from a foundation that helped Christian organizations.

After explaining our dilemma with the head man of the foundation, he simply asked me, "Why is your church any different from any other who comes asking for financial help?" It was quite obvious to me why we were different but to him we seemed the same.

All the way back to the office I repeated this statement to the Lord, "Why are we different?"

We were having revival. People's lives were being changed; mothers and fathers were leaving their drugs behind; children were actually being visited by the Lord; and their parents were coming to church; supernatural answers were coming for desperate situations; the unchurched were coming; people were being discipled to take the Gospel to their friends; on-the-spot healings were taking place; people were getting off of welfare and finding hope for the future and a reason for living. It was wonderful!

After all that tirade going off in my mind, a little thought was able to creep into my thinking. "Check the records."

I always felt that the way we prayed was different. It was not the usual. We actually acted it out as if we were killing the giants in the land. We used the same stone (imagined) that David used to kill Goliath. We actually wrote job orders out to get new parts for arthritic joints or new hearts or whatever was needed and sent it off to the Lord by burning it up. More important, we believed that Jesus was present right there with us as we prayed. The results were a new heart, cancer left, warts fell off, broken bones were healed, spine straitened, marriages healed, house returned to family and more.

Who would have the records of giants falling? I called the police and found out that records were kept and that

Tacoma was gridded off. Any crime committed in a certain grid would be credited with that crime. All this information was at the Library and I was free to check it out. I found out that our targeted area was in two Tacoma grids plus University Place.

It seemed complicated at first, but when I got the idea I went over the statistics for the years before we showed up and during the time we started praying for our area. And this is what I found out—CRIME AND VANDALISM went down in our targeted area. I also found out that CRIME AND VANDALISM went up in the areas around our targeted area and in most all other grids in Tacoma. So there it was. We were a different kind of church! Spiritual Principalities were coming down.

Another reason our church was different was when our church moved to 56th and Orchard we landed right in the middle of apartment city. Kids were all over the place going in all directions. The apartment managers had opened arms for our after school program. Right after the kids got off of the school bus we were there with an hour of fun and games.

This program was very successful to get the children interested in the Wednesday night 'Live Wire' program and eventually getting their parents into church. It only took two people and five days on each apartment campus to draw in five or six children. There were sixteen apartments within a four-block radius of our church.

One particular mother saw our flyer on the rec-room bulletin board and gathered all the kids in her apartment complex, even though she was totally spaced out on drugs, a confession she made after she was delivered, born again, baptized, and healed.

It was interesting to see how a family of four girls, ages sixteen to twenty, a fourteen-year-old son and a mother could all live in a two bedroom, small apartment. Not on welfare, the mother cleaned homes, the two older girls found "Oshkosh" baby clothes at Value Mart for one dollar, cleaned and repaired them and sold them for five dollars. Somehow this covered their living costs. Because of divorce, this was a displaced Catholic family that loved attending our church because "Jesus was there".

How do you minister to a perky, petite Baptist mother of five from five different husbands, and the one she was living with now wasn't her husband? The four older children were old before their age, doing things that could only lead to destruction. The six-year-old was the one we concentrated on. The mother told me later that her daughter came home and told her she saw Jesus while walking to church. From that point on she was a regular little missionary bringing as many kids as she could to church.

Some of us would make two or three trips to pick up the kids and bring them to club. The amazing thing about this program was that the kids and Jesus became close friends.

One new face was so concerned about her mother that every time she came she wanted prayer for her. She lived with her father and his new wife while her mother had a live-in, drug-addicted boy friend. She had seen her mother beaten black and blue by the live-in. When the seven-year-old came back after a three-week absence, she took me aside to tell me the story of what happened to her mother. She had taken the little "One Way" booklet telling the Gospel story of Jesus and shared it with her mother. Her mother responded to the message and promised her daughter she would attend church the next Sunday. For her mother, next Sunday never came. The boy friend, high on drugs, ran her car into a telephone pole killing her mother. As tragic as that story was, it really was an answer to prayer for the seven-year-old's family. Such pain!

While playing games with the kids at one apartment campus, I heard my name being called from a second-story balcony, "Mrs. Schmidtke." A young pregnant mother with two preschool children was waving enthusiastically at me. I recognized her as a former Junior High student from my teaching years. Too embarrassed to let me into her apartment, we sat on the upper steps and talked about her life and what had happened. A failed marriage with two small children, an out-of-wedlock pregnancy by someone else and a family that wouldn't speak to her because of her rebellious life style, left her struggling like most of the others we worked with.

As we sat there talking, her next door neighbor came out in all of his transvestite apparel. This was a healthy good-looking young man underneath all the glaring make up who needed to experience the reality of Jesus.

So many of these young adults were reliving the Prodigal son story. Even the pig pen smells would take my breath away as I visited with the parents of the kids we ministered to. Two-thirds of the apartments were filled with unwed mothers hoping upon hope that their "knight in shining armor" would come and sweep them off their feet. They laid down their bodies for this hope only to find themselves expecting another child and the seed-planter gone.

I would like to share the story of Angela, the mother of two wonderful young girls who attended Live Wire. As the door opened to my knock, a bright, clear eyed, well-dressed mother greeted me with a "won't you come in?" Most of the doors I knocked on opened just a crack and some didn't open at all. Sharing the Gospel with Angela wasn't as easy as I thought it would be. Several days after our visit the newspaper told the story of this family's tragedy. It seems that her boyfriend would use her as a punching bag. And this particular night he came home to do it again. She ran to the bedroom, locked the door just in time to keep his pounding fist to the door. On the bed was his gun that was part of his uniform as an army M.P.. Fearing for her life, she shot through the door wounding him. Her two girls were in the living room and could see the results of the bullets hitting the boyfriend. As she opened the door, she continued to empty the rest of the bullets into his body.

The next time I saw her she was in jail. As she came into the room, she was a broken woman. Everything was taken away from her. Her girls went to live with their father fifteen hundred miles away. Not a friend, relative or a family member lived near enough to visit. She was truly alone. Now she was ready to hear about Jesus. She best describes her story in a letter she sent to me dated 12/4/93.

Dear Pastor Kathy,

Thank you for giving me God's word I'm finally born again. I'm a true Christian. Praise God!

Pastor Kathy, I remember the day you came to my home and spoke to me about accepting Jesus. I told you that I was already a Christian, but I wasn't and you knew. Because if that was so I wouldn't have been living the way I was, a sinful life style. For to love Christ is to hate sin. God has forgiven me all. He has created in me a new spirit! I now can face my future no matter what. Jesus is walking with me. Thank you for this wonderful life line. My little red Bible!

One day when all this I must endure will be over, I will have a Christian home. I have a testimony. I am witnessing to my fellow inmates. I want to share my joy! Jesus is our only Savior. Thank you Jesus! Praise God. Pastor Kathy, for the first time in my life I understand God's word. The Holy Spirit is teaching me more and more every day. God's word is my life-line. I take of it every day. I'm praying constantly for the will to apply God's word always to my life.

God has blessed me and answers so many of my prayers thus far. Thank you for leading me this way. I know my Father sent you. All glory be to God!

Love. God Bless You. Angela"

Violet became an unusual helper when we first started our Live Wire program. She was a former bouncer, physically built to do the job and very attractive at the same time. She saw our announcement on the rec-room bulletin board of her complex and was the instigator of rounding up kids, as well as her own, to attend. She would always retreat into her darkened apartment when we came. I was always looking for helpers so, I went to visit. Ninety-nine percent of the time when you knock on apartment doors, they open a crack. It is a dark world inside. Violet was living in sin but, she wanted something better for her kids. She was totally controlled by a married man from another town who would come with drugs and take what he wanted from her. Eventually she started coming to church with her kids. She gave her heart to the Lord the very first Sunday. Her boyfriend had a definite hold on her, but eventually with the help of the Holy Spirit she told him to leave. Strange things started happening in her apartment; even the kids were scarred. The guy wasn't about to leave and continued to harass her by phone. She agreed to clear the house out of everything he had given to her family. The spiritual tie she had with this guy was broken once she cleared his things out and for three months they were free. Violet called one evening wanting me to come over and pray for her apartment. There was something strange going on. She had run water for a bath and felt what she thought was a hand going down her body. This was not a physical person but something spooky. I told her that Satan couldn't enter her house unless she still had something there that God didn't approve of. It has to be something pornographic. Sure enough, she found an unmarked porno video tape that the boyfriend had brought into her home. Once it was destroyed, we anointed her home with oil and they were never bothered again. She did a most unusual thing in both looking for a husband and sharing the Gospel at the same time. A newspaper blind date would have to meet her at our church Sunday morning. She was looking for a husband; they, it turns out, were looking for something else. It was kind of fun watching them when the power of God moved. As Violet grew stronger in the Lord, she and her kids decided to move back to Oregon where she cared for her ailing grandmother.

Now, Lovena's mother was the exception. Her home was clean and neat, curtains opened, clothes clean and put in their place. This mother brought her daughter to church, participated in the women's Bible study and seemed like she was on the right path. Abandoned by her family, and no support from the father of her child caused Lovena's mother to use survival skills that only took her into deeper waters. Several years later I found out that she had another child out of wedlock and no husband.

Young mothers, with no high school diploma, divorced or deserted by their boyfriends, seemed to be overwhelmed by the situation. That is why we went right on the apartment campuses and offered classes on Getting off of welfare and back to work, Parenting, Budgeting and Nutrition. We were having revival! People's lives were being changed: mothers and fathers were leaving their drugs behind; children were actually being visited by the Lord; and their parents were coming to church; supernatural answers were coming for desperate situations; the unchurched were coming; people were being discipled to take the Gospel to their friends; on the-spot healings were taking place; people were getting off of welfare and finding hope for the future and a reason for living.

A Korean mother married a career service man, left her home land and family, came to the United States, had a son and when the son became a teenager she could not handle him. He had been incarcerated several times. The father was off on tour duty in Arabia so he was no help. It was at this time in her life that we met. To be alone in a foreign country without any family or friends was very difficult for her. When her son was young and manageable she put all of her energies in on his welfare and upbringing. She could speak English, but reading the Bible was another matter. Attending a Korean church was not something she wanted to do, so we learned to struggle together. Eventually, she gave her heart to Jesus, was filled with the Holy Spirit and started bringing people to church. It was quite amazing to see her grow in the Lord.

Her son, however, was another matter. An emergency call came into the office wanting me to do something about her son who had run away. I tried contacting my son who was the Campus Life Director for YFC and assistant pastor at our church, but he was not available at the time to give assistance, so, I responded. When I entered her apartment, she was mad at God, her husband, the social system and just generally mad. As she stomped back and forth across the room the thought occurred to me that she had gone a little batty. He hair was flying, no longer controlled by the metal clip which just missed me as it flew through the air to hit the window. Any help that I offered was not what she wanted to hear. So, I thought it was time for me to leave, until she calmed down a bit. I excused myself and told her I would be glad to pray with her when she was more receptive. When I got into the car my conversation to the Lord was 'This lady is out of order. She is really ranting and raving.'. And the Lord's response to me was 'That was you last night'.

What a way to let me know my actions were observed by the Lord. My encounter with this lady was truly a mirrored reflection of what went on in my livingroom the night before. This revelation brought me to my knees. My desperation or frustration the night before had to do with the money God had promised to bring in and the lack of it.

WHERE WAS THE MONEY?

In starting this new work in the Chambers Creek area I was promised seven million dollars from two different sources each responding to a prospectus I had sent out telling of the vision and dream for the Chambers Creek area. At first the report was sent out to ten people explaining the need for seed money of three and a half million dollars. The owners would not separate the 'pair of boots' property from the acreage above, so, the tag for both pieces was two million dollars for sixty-four acres. The one and a half million we could use to do the preparation work of the land and then sell the above property to start our church with a 'sprung' building holding three hundred seats, followed by the high school at seven hundred and fifty students, then on to building the three thousand seat church. Quite a marvelous idea!

God was truly fulfilling his promise of bringing in the money: two of the ten who responded, each was willing to give three and a half million dollars, 'even if my wife and I have to go into our own personal finances'. As the weeks, months and years went by this promised money was always just around the corner. The frustration with these two separate millionaires was that they always left me with a ray of hope that the money would actually come.

I had a few hoops to go through with the one financier. Bellarmine High School held the office of the head of the Pierce County private school honcho, and he wanted me to talk with him. Our talks were interesting, but pointless because I wouldn't be responsible for that part of our project. I had a niece and nephew who were both principals of schools in Oregon waiting in the wings to be called forward when the time was right.

In 1990 we put our sign on the property: "Future home of Chambers Creek Assembly of God". The promissory note was signed with the owners. The pressure was now on to get the money or loose the twelve thousand dollar's earnest money. I kept reminding myself—this is God's idea, not mine, I was just the vessel that He was using to get His work accomplished. I sent hundreds of prospectuses out after researching the books for foundations who would be interested in giving start-up money for this project. The grant applications they sent back to be filled out were one major pain, each one different from the other. In the first place these foundations had their own pet projects they were involved in. I spent hours filling out grant applications only to get it rejected with a postcard. Why did God give me this idea and not bring the money in?

I had an opportunity to talk with a former neighbor who was the director of a foundation that gave away millions of dollars a year. He got me an interview with the new director. "Now the way this works is that you have a large body of believers first, then you ask for money." I was more of the philosophy "If you build it they will come."

There were wonderful little reminders along the way that God was still in control. One time when I was getting rather discouraged I was called by a young mother who was going to the Philippines on a missionary trip with her seven-year-old son and asked me if I would come over and pray for her son who was having leg problems. I did and he immediately went to sleep on the couch while she and I continued to talk about what God was doing in our lives. Like a sleep walker the boy rose up from his reclined position and said 'You will get the money to build the Church. Fear not!" And laid back down sound asleep. That little experience was like new adrenaline to keep us going. The request for funds continued, including the two financiers who kept me hanging by a hair.

It was one thing to ask for money from a foundation but it was a whole different experience to ask wealthy individuals to part with their money. I asked one lady who buried a million dollars in the backyard, and when she was ready to move she had no idea where it was. It would cost her fifty percent of what one person would charge to find it. She got her own Geiger counter system and located it.

My wealthy, newly widowed friend, who was with me when I had my burning bush experience, did not jump in like I would have hoped. She went to college and got her doctorate degree and died of a blood disease shortly thereafter, her money ending up in a court battle.

On one side it looked like I was a representative of God, here on earth, letting people know how they could get involved with a wonderful plan to build a church, high school and center: and on the other hand, it looked to some like I was begging for money for my own project.

Oh, the joy of putting our sign up for all the world to see and the absolute downer when we had to remove it after our nine months. We lost the twelve thousand dollars earnest money but counted it as seed planted. When a person is led by a dream and a vision, defeat doesn't enter into your thinking; you know that God is in control and the answer will come. In fact, just shortly after having to take our sign down and making another call to my friend in Seattle— a promise was given, that within the next three months the money we needed would be ours. We were excited but cautious at the same time for this was the same person who assured us the money would be there in the beginning.

Chapter 12

WHAT HAPPENED, LORD?

N ew couples started coming to the store front church on 56th and Orchard who were new to the area and ready to learn about the Lord. These were young babes in the knowledge of the Lord, experiencing real miracles, healings, deliverance, financial blessings, jobs, families reunited, marriages healed and wanting everything the Lord had to offer. They were like dried-up sponges just sucking it up and wanting to share everything they were learning with others. Great friendships were made during this time, and we became a close family of believers. One family in particular was very creative in keeping afloat financially until the husband found a job. They had three children of their own and took in three foster children. The youngest of the fostered children had a bad case of asthma and was dramatically healed before church service. When the healing took place, her eyes got big, she took in a great breath and jumped for joy. She was three years old and spoke only Spanish so she was scared when we started to pray for her, but what a smile she had when her breathing came. The foster mother was healed of a leg-joint problem and the foster father was healed of an eye injury.

Several things started to happen simultaneously during this period of time. Because of the tremendous healings that were taking place at our church one of the fathers, who had received the eye healing, spoke of it to the warehousemen that he worked with. They were curious to know who the pastor was. When he said it was Pastor Kathy, they were quick to show him scriptures in the Bible where women were not to teach men nor to be pastors. Four of our new families met in his home while his pastor came over and went through the scriptures that he believed kept women out of the ministry. The next Sunday four families were attending the other pastor's church. This was a mighty blow to our church family for these were our workers (nursery school teacher, high school teacher, musicians, janitor and prayer warriors), financial supporters, and eager beavers to share the gospel with others. It didn't matter that five months later two of the families called and wanted to know where we were holding church.

We had been at our location fourteen months when we received a notification from the owners that we would have to be out in a month's time or pay the regular monthly charge of three thousand dollars for the two sections that we used. Not only that, but we would have to sign a lease for five years. The owner graciously allowed us to stay for four more months at the regular five hundred dollars.

It never entered my mind that we were to close our church doors. And because of that I made another attempt at getting the funds from the two people who had promised, four years earlier, their financial support that would get us on the property and in the building. My college friend was so disturbed at my coming again he had his lawyer write me a letter to stop, even though, he himself told me when he sold his radio stations he would give me a call.

Interesting thing about the 'pair of boots' property; we never gave up hope, even after we had to close our doors at 56th and Orchard. The six previous moves were always accompanied by the Lord giving explicit directions to the next destination and we hoped number seven would be on the property at 67th and Bridgeport Way.

Chapter 13

CLOSING THE DOORS

On November 1, 1993, after four wonderful years of ministering in the Chambers Creek area, we gave our furniture and blue chairs to another church and we made sure our remaining people were attending churches that would meet their needs. A lack of funds would seem like the reason for our having to close, but now, I believe that it was the Lord who took us through these experiences in order to expose an enemy. The enemy is a philosophy that must be stopped dead in its tracks. And that philosophy is the belief that women are not welcome, wanted or needed in church leadership.

The story can best be told by someone who has lived through the fallout of this philosophy. And what makes it so difficult to expose is that it is fellow workers in the ministry that are espousing this philosophy: people who are called of

God. It is not my purpose to expose people, but to expose a philosophy that is detrimental to the work of the ministry of Jesus Christ.

The hedge is down—the protective shield is broken with such a philosophy as gender bias being preached from the pulpit and lived out by the leaders of the church.

This is the very breach in the protective hedge that the fiery darts of Satan can come through and damage the church body. And what damage has been done; a senator falls, a church planter dies, dementia strikes, an inheritance is wasted, incurable blood disease kills, a church closes, multitudes of souls lost to the kingdom of Satan and it goes on.

How long can this philosophy continue? It must stop now. To continue with this thinking delays the spread of the gospel message and its ability to change people's lives. How devastating to be a part of this carnage. To be helpless to help those who are at the edge of destruction because of a philosophy that feeds ego, pride and chauvinistic behavior, is without honor.

Our society is a mirrored reflection of what has gone wrong in the church. What the church leaders believe and act out, our society reveals. And what does our society show us? Gender bias in the church causes our society to reflect: Disrespect for women, paid less for the same job, passed over when it comes to promotions, treated as sexual objects, discarded when something better comes along, physically and mentally abused, required to submit to male authority and pleasures, changed life styles, same-gender marriages, prostitution, live-in boy friends, sexual perversions of all types, and it goes on.

For me to say this so boldly carries with it the possibility of being called a feminist.

But, I am not alone in this thinking, for the Bible says in Hosea 4:6 "My people are destroyed because they don't know me, and it is all your fault, you priests, for you yourselves refuse to know me."

This scripture points out that what you see happening in a society, good or bad, can be accredited to the leaders, in this case the priests.

It isn't society that holds the key to restoration for the land, it is the "my people who are called by my name" that make the difference. 2 Chronicles 7:14 says "If my people, which are called by my name, shall humble themselves, and pray, and seek my face and turn from their wicked ways: then will I hear from heaven, and will forgive their sin, and will heal their land." (KJV)

It starts with the leaders of the church. Let us wake up. Let us reverence what God has created and respect his creation. Down with the philosophy of gender bias, and let us join together as partners—team players in the task that is set before us. We are not to wrestle against flesh and blood, but, we wrestle against spiritual principalities. To have to struggle against friendly fire in order to fulfil the higher call of God on our life puts us in remembrance of what Judas did to Jesus.

Chapter 14

JESUS SUPPORTS WOMEN IN THE MINISTRY

When I had my little chat with the Lord during the burning bush experience, I asked Him who would be the pastor of the church. His replay was, "You will." My response had a lot to do with my upbringing and popular opinion, "Why would you pick a woman?" His answer came back with, "I didn't pick a woman. I picked a vessel. Any more than I pick a man." That settled that at the time, but when you get into the world of male headship philosophy, a person runs into problems with both male and female folks having to do with women pastors. I am very well acquainted with the scriptures that are used to keep women out of certain rolls in the ministry. And in my humble opinion, when it is used against women in the ministry, it has more to do with pride, gender bias, territorialism and jealousy—not scripture. J. Lee Grady, editor of Charisma magazine, has written a book entitled "10 LIES THE CHURCH TELLS WOMEN." (How the Bible has been misused to keep women in spiritual bondage). The Assembly of God ordains women and emphasizes Gal 3:28 as their basis. It would be nice to see a few more women on their leadership boards, however.

Let's look at what Jesus has to say about this subject of women in the ministry. I believe He is the highest authority.

Matthew 28:9-10: "And as they (the women) were running, suddenly Jesus was there in front of them! 'Good morning!' he said. And they fell to the ground before him, holding his feet and worshiping him. Then Jesus said to them, 'Don't be frightened! Go tell my brothers to leave at once for Galilee, to meet me there.'"(TLB)

It's quite obvious that Jesus trusts and gives women the authority to deliver a message to the disciples—the leaders of the church at that time.

In the next scripture, we find that Jesus is not to happy with his leaders for not believing the chosen messengers, who just happened to be women, and rebukes them for their stubborn unbelief.

Mark 16:14: "Still later he appeared to the eleven disciples as they were eating together. He rebuked them for their unbelief —their stubborn refusal to believe those who had seen him alive from the dead."(TLB)

The King James Version is even more descriptive with the words "and upbraided them with their unbelief and hardness of heart..."

In Revelation 2:20-21 Jesus has a perfect opportunity for all time to keep women out of the preaching role if that was his decree with the story of Jezebel. "Yet I have this against you: You are permitting that woman Jezebel, who calls herself a prophetess, to teach my servants that sex sin is not a serious matter; she urges them to practice immorality and to eat meat that has been sacrificed to idols. **I gave her time to change her mind and attitude**, but she refused."(NIV—TLB)

Notice that Jesus didn't say, get that woman out of there because she was usurping authority over men or that she was in the ministry. No, it was her message that was wrong. She was told to change her message. He gave her time to change her message. You don't give a person time to change a message if your purpose is to get her out of the ministry.

In the case of Mary and Martha, found in Luke 10:39, we have another example of a woman more concerned about listening to Jesus:

"Her sister Mary sat on the floor, listening to Jesus as he talked. But Martha was the jittery type, and was worrying over the big dinner she was preparing.

She came to Jesus and said, 'Sir, doesn't it seem unfair to you that my sister just sits here while I do all the work? Tell her to come and help me.'

But the Lord said to her, 'Martha, dear friend, you are so upset over all these details! There is really only one thing worth being concerned about. Mary has discovered it—and

I won't take it away from her!'"(TLB)

Martha wanted to take Mary's calling away from her and felt she had a right to do it. So, what is the advice for today?

If you don't like women in the ministry, take your complaint to Jesus and hear him say, "Mary has discovered her ministry and I won't take it away from her."

Jesus tells both men and women to be filled with the Holy Spirit before they go out to minister.

Acts 1:4 (referring to Jesus' statements)—"He told them not to leave Jerusalem until the Holy Spirit came upon them in fulfillment of the Father's promise, a matter he had previously discussed with them."(TLB)

Acts 1:8 (referring to Jesus' statements)—"But when the Holy Spirit has come upon you, you will receive power to testify about me with great effect, to the people in Jerusalem, throughout Judea, in Samaria, and to the ends of the earth, about my death and resurrection."(TLB)

These statements were and are directed to men and women of yesterday and today. Why should women be filled with the Holy Spirit if the gifts of the Holy Spirit will be wasted on someone who is not allowed to minister. The gifts are for ministry and not to be wasted.

Let's get real. Once you are filled with the Holy Spirit, you can't remain quiet. To have the experience of being born again and then filled with the Holy Spirit causes such a desire to proclaim the Gospel it can't be held back.

Men and women were up in the Upper room on the day of Pentecost and all were filled with the Holy Spirit. There was no gender discrimination in that meeting nor is there today.

Acts 1:2-4—"Suddenly there was a sound like the roaring of a mighty windstorm in the skies above them and it filled the house where they were meeting. Then, what looked like flames or tongues of fire appeared and settled on their heads. And everyone present was filled with the Holy Spirit and began speaking in languages they didn't know, for the Holy Spirit gave them this ability."(TLB)

I tell you when the Holy Spirit fills you he gives you abilities that are spiritual and come out of a vessel, whether male or female.

And anyone who talks against the Holy Spirit is looking for deep trouble.

Matthew 12:32—"And whosoever speaketh a word against the Son of man , it shall be forgiven him: but whosoever speaketh against the Holy Ghost, it shall not be forgiven him, neither in this world, neither in the world to come." (KJV)

Prophesied in Joel and manifested in Acts 2:16-18 is the manifesto for all believers.

Acts 2:16-18—"What you see this morning was predicted centuries ago by the prophet Joel— 'In the last days,' God said, 'I will pour out my Holy Spirit upon all mankind, and your sons and daughters shall prophesy, and your young men shall see visions, and your old men dream dreams. Yes, the Holy Spirit shall come upon all my servants, men and women alike, and they shall prophesy." (TLB)

That seems pretty clear to me. The Holy Spirit is the one

who gives us (men and women) the dreams and visions and direction for our lives. Why would we want to come against the Holy Spirit?

Paul has some interesting things to say about women and all of them must agree with what Jesus has to say.

Check out Gal. 3:27-28—"...and we who have been baptized into union with Christ are enveloped by him. We are no longer Jews or Greeks or slaves or free men or even merely men or women, but we are all the same—we are Christians; we are one in Christ Jesus."(TLB)

This is clear enough. When we look at our Christian brothers and sisters, we should be seeing the envelopment of Jesus all over them.

When we see women and men as physical beings we see differences and that is the only way the secular or carnal world sees and treats women. How you see men or women is a carnal or spiritual revelation. The 'born again' believer must start seeing as Jesus describes His sons and daughters.

Gal 2:20—"I am crucified with Christ: nevertheless I live; yet not I, but Christ lives in me: and the life which I now live in the flesh I live by the faith of the Son of God, who loved me, and gave himself for me." (KJV)

That describes what happened to me. I 'died' at the age of 30. The old me died and was of no value to the Lord, but it is a different story today. I am His friend called to do what he would have me do.

When Jesus selects vessels to propagate His story to the lost, who are we to usurp authority over the Lord's directive.

He would even say why are you persecuting my people.

Acts 9:1-6—"But Paul, threatening with every breath and eager to destroy every Christian, went to the High Priest in Jerusalem. He requested a letter addressed to synagogues in Damascus, requiring their cooperation in the persecution of any believers he found there, both men and <u>women</u>, so that he could bring them in chains to Jerusalem.

As he was nearing Damascus on this mission, suddenly a brilliant light from heaven spotted down upon him! He fell to the ground and heard a voice saying to him, 'Paul! Paul! Why are you persecuting me?' 'Who is speaking, sir?' Paul asked. And the voice replied, 'I am Jesus, the one you are persecuting!'"(TLB)

There you have it. Jesus himself makes it clear that persecuting believers is an attack upon him, no matter what the sex. Paul ended up blind for three days. It is nice to know that Paul got the message and stopped persecuting the believers and became one himself.

The question is "Can that happen today?" The great desire of the Father, Son and Holy Spirit is that everyone will come to the saving knowledge of the Gospel. It was and still is the assignment for every Christian to preach the Good News in season and out when it is convenient and when it is not.

Listen to Jesus in Luke 16:15-18: "And then he told them, 'You are to go into all the world and preach the Good News to everyone, everywhere. Those who believe and are baptized will be saved. But those who refuse to believe will be condemned. And those who believe shall use my authority to cast out demons, and they shall speak new languages. They will be able even to handle snakes with safety, and if they drink anything poisonous, it won't hurt them; and they will be able to place their hands on the sick and heal them.'"

Chapter 15

RESPONSES THAT LEAD TO TRAGIC RESULTS

I t is rather significant to note that every person that heard or read the burning bush story, knew that it was from God. The fact that the dream and vision were tied into the map and the property, was definitely the kind of thing the Lord would do. The following stories have become important to report, whether coincidental or supernatural, because they point out the character and philosophies of believers. Why then, these responses that led to such tragic results? Have some of the leaders of the church propagated the wrong message? Have we forgotten the mission of the church, the task that we have all been called to do?

Casualty #1

The first one I called about this project listened quietly and patiently while I told of the burning bush experience I had with the Lord when I was in England in 1988 at a Rienhart Bonnke convention showing me in a vision the plot of land in Tacoma that I was to build a church, high school and center on. The whole story took about eight minutes.

This was a man who was a mover and a shaker in the Christian community and a State worker. He and my husband grew up in the same church: we were in the same adult Sunday school class together, surely he would be a great help to propel this project forward.

His response pierced my heart. **"Do you know what they did in the Old Testament to faults prophets?"** "No, what do you mean?" **"They stoned them!"** The moment he made that comment to me, the thought ran through my head, "The stones will fall on you. You have ensnared yourself with these words. Can't you tell this project is of the Lord?"

Surely he was joking. Surely he could see the finger prints of God on the vision and dream. Why would he take this attitude? I had forgotten that he didn't believe God could possibly use a woman in the ministry. Women were to stay home for the beckoned call of their husband and kids and be ornaments on their arms.

I remembered his comment so clearly one year later when the newspaper, radio and TV ran the story; 'Senator is being accused of sexual harassment by his secretary.' He left the Senate a disgraced man.

Casualty #2

I called upon another friend from our former church, a very wealthy man who had been instrumental in starting several churches in the surrounding area. His philosophy was very similar to the Senator's with an added zinger. Speaking in tongues was not for today and he would not support a project that fell under that spell.

After we had closed our church doors, I was talking to mutual friends and I found out that three days after his negative response to my request, he had died. He was on his way to work when he had a massive heart attack while driving his car. This was confirmed after reviewing my date book of our meeting.

At first it was hard for me to connect these stories, nor did I think that there was any possible connection. When I heard about these tragedies, I thought of them as ordinary consequences of life.

Casualty #3

There was one particular man that had been in my growth classes who was a wonderful altar worker, telephone counselor and moved on to become a deacon of the church. He didn't like women in the ministry. When my family and I went out to start the new church, he spoke negatively about my becoming an active pastor. I learned later that just shortly after we left he had a brain tumor which was successfully removed, but left him with dementia. One of his best friends told me years later more of the details having to do with his philosophy about women in the ministry. Men were to be the head. It is kind of interesting to note that it was the head that was affected.

There is a job to be done to get the lost into the Kingdom of God and it is going to take all of us—men and women alike. We must work together as team members: partners with Jesus at the head giving the directions.

Casualty #4

It was in 1988 that my friend and I went to Birmingham, England to be part of Reinhardt Bonnke's seminar to the Evangelist of Europe. It was at 3:00 a.m. in the morning when I had my "burning bush" experience about the "pair of boots". My friend was a light sleeper and she told me later she could tell something was going on. In the morning I wrote the experience down. It was something that I was not ready to share in detail with anyone because I wasn't aware or sure of the significance of the whole thing.

The minute I told my friend that I had an experience with the Lord of a scroll unrolling and showing me a plot of land in Tacoma and actually talking for about an hour about a project He had in mind for the Chambers Creek area, she got a bit upset with me. She had always been a wonderful partner. We had great times together. This was a whole new side of her that I didn't understand until later.

She went back to school and I didn't see her for a long time. It was during this time that I looked into the property. Was it there, was it available, did my kids believe the story, did they want to get involved, would others believe and want to help? Yes, was the response to all of the above. For myself, I fluctuated between "yes, I'll do it" and "no, this couldn't be happening." This was a 15 million-dollar project; where would I get that kind of money?

I knew my friend would be home from school so I called her and asked her if she would accompany me to a church just beyond Kirkland. It was at this time that I shared the whole experience of the dream, vision and the map that showed the 'pair of boots' in hopes she would want to be part of this project. She was a multimillionaire, about to graduate from Northwest College and was praying that God would show her what she was to do with the rest of her life. After all she was with me at the conception of this miracle, at least she knew that it wasn't hokey.

"I'll pray for you, Kathy, but I won't get involved." Her response came at me rather cold and sterile, not what I had hoped for nor expected. I knew that getting the money and the people was the Lord's responsibility but surely he wanted to use my friend in this project.

Again, I didn't see my friend after that for a long time. We started the church, and she went all over the states to get her graduate's degree. The next time I saw her was at her wedding. A very sick woman. She had a mysterious blood disease that she confided to me in order that I might pray for her. After her marriage I tried to call, but the phone calls, I later found out, were not passed on to her. She was closed off to all of her friends. Never the less I tried to contact her.

Before she died, she confessed to me that she was jealous of me and my relationship with the Lord. Why hadn't God given her a vision? We had a good cry over that one. The millions of dollars she had, ended up in a court fight over whom it would belong to.

I suppose this one was the most devastating to me because we were such great friends. We were friends, Danish, about the same age and Christians. You just don't find that combination too often. I am confident that she would be alive and well today, building a church, high school, and center with us if jealousy hadn't popped its ugly head in.

Casualty #5

When I went to talk to the owners of the property, I told the older brother the whole unusual story of the dream and vision in hopes of stopping this whole process, but it didn't have that effect on him. He let me know that they were just recently in the process of dividing up the property and he took me all over the hundreds of acres asking me which part I wanted.

I kept checking in with the owners to see what was going on with the property. It couldn't last forever. It was like a rosebud when we went out to start the church and then started to bloom with the surrounding acreage being sold, and filled with lovely new homes.

Where does the money come from for such a project as this? Even though the Lord said he would bring the money in, I frustrated over the fact that we needed it right away. Some people's comments were of no help at all, 'If God is in it, He will provide.' Others expected the money to float down from Heaven, or this may not be God's will for this time—you know His time and our time are not the same.' For lots of reasons those comments were not helpful.

In the dream the Lord gave me, He said to get or buy a pair of boots. We did our best to buy it. Perhaps the brothers would give it to us. At the next meeting, in desperation, I asked if they would like to give the property to our church. The older brother was not against this idea, but he pointed out that the younger brother wanted the money.

The next meeting I was told the younger brother was dying of an incurable disease and I was not to come back unless I had the money. The end.

My grandson, who was twelve at the time, had a visitation from the Lord. His experience came the day after I had finished a three-day fast. I finished on Thursday without any results to the two questions I placed before the Lord. It was my weekend to have the boys at my house. While I was fixing dinner, he came in, sat down at the table and preceded to tell me of his experience with Jesus. Jesus told him to take a nap and he would visit him. After lunch Jesus walked into his bedroom surrounded by a bright light and told him, 'Tell your grandmother she is going to get the land and the church'. Boy, did I drop everything. He got the third degree questioning from me. He answered the two questions I fasted and prayed for.

New hope emerges. I decided to talk to the owners of the property once again. The thought occurred to me, perhaps the Lord would heal the younger brother if I went over and laid hands on him. Then maybe he could see that God was in this project and would give us the property. I decided to take the challenge. They were both there. The younger one had lost a lot of weight but he was still alive. The older one asked what I wanted. **"The pair of boots", is it still available?"** "Have you got the money?" **"No, but I have an idea. Maybe God will heal your brother...."**

Before I could finish that statement, the younger brother reported that he was already healed. His son had given him one of his kidneys. I looked at his arm and could see underneath his flesh a large snake like plastic tube going up the arm into his body.

As I left, I wondered if this all could have been avoided if he had just been willing to give the property to the Lord. The value of just the 'pair of boots' property would have been about eight hundred thousand dollars at the time we were asking. A person would have to have a good reason to donate such a gift.

Casualty #6

In sharing this story with people who have the money, there is always the possibility that someone will decide to buy it for themselves and use it for their own purpose. It would seem rather risky for someone to do that, but some people try. One famous saying was "The window of opportunity doesn't last forever." The question is, "do you have to worry about that when God is in it?" I had to take the risk and leave the results in God's hands.

As the surrounding property was being purchased and homes were being built on the land, I would constantly keep an eye on any movement on the property. Talking to the owners was out. They didn't want to see me unless I had the money.

Eight months went by without any word from the Lord. I went to the County City Land Department and found out that someone had house plotted the property that was hooked up to the "pair of boots". My heart sank into my stomach. Never before had the owners been willing to separate the two pieces. Anyone wanting the upper piece had to take the "pair of boots", or vice versa.

Was it over for us? I found out the name of the construction company that was involved. It was not familiar to me. I called the company to find out the name of the owner. The news both saddened me and gave me hope at the same time. The name of the owner I knew. I had sent him a request for finances letter telling of this project, its location and its significant to the Christian world. The sad part was that he decided he would take the property and use it for his project. He had a heart attack during this time and had to drop the property like a hot potato. So hope for the church was still alive.

Why was it important for me to find this out? Why couldn't God just allow the money to come in and let us get on with the task of building His church?

No doubt about it, jealousy, territorial giants, pride and the fact that God couldn't possibly use a woman as a minister, constantly tried to bully into the forefront. I am beginning to think these positions are dangerous for Christians to have.

Casualty # 7

The father who was healed so miraculously of eye problems opened up a can of worms in his enthusiasm to share with others his story. He was bombarded with the traditional comments; occult church, get out quick, women aren't to teach men, they can't be pastors. This philosophy pulled his family and three other families with him into a church whose pastor believed that Jesus's commission to take the Gospel to the world was just for the men disciples, not for women, that dreams and visions were just for old men and boys, not for women, that women were not to teach men.

Three months later two of the families called and wanted to come back. At the same time, I learned that the family that had the eye healing was no longer a family. The husband lost his job, stopped going to church all together, started using drugs and walked away from his family. The pastor who so badly mangled scripture was on local TV as host, confessing he had been and was still in depression and wanted prayer. Was this the heavy toll of a biased philosophy?

Casualty #8

The woman who fell down the stairs was like a mirrored reflection casualty. This very wealthy lady was once a neighbor of mine and we had lots of conversations about wanting to help support the Lords' work, so I felt I could send her a prospectus of our project. I usually followed up the mail-out with a phone call, but her number was unlisted. I was ringing her door bell when she and her son drove up. She had to walk up her steps to get to the front door. I waited for her at the door. She didn't recognize me at first so her comment to me was rather terse. **'What do you want?'** 'It's me, Kathy. I am following up on the 'pair of boots' project.' **'I don't have any money.'** The son's response was, 'Oh, Mom, why are you saying that?' She said it again. The son just looked at his mother. 'It's O.K. I understand. My job is to tell the story in hopes that people will see that this is God's project, not mine, and want to respond.'

I went home and told the Lord we struck out. Now what do we do? The next week I ran into one of her friends as we were headed out to our cars. She proceeded to tell me that our friend had fallen backwards, tumbling over and over all the way down the basement stairs at her son's home, breaking ribs, bones, head bumps and bruises. The son tried desperately to stop the fall. Their dog had rushed by and thrown her off balance and there was nothing he could do. Not only was the mother in bad shape but the son was traumatized by the whole experience of having to watch his mother fall and not be able to do anything about it. Sort of a strange reversal of what happened just four days before—an opportunity to do something great for the Lord. Sad for everyone concerned.

I would like to think that these casualties were simply coincidental happenings, everyday occurrences, having nothing to do with anything. But there are more and when the details are known there is less doubt.

There are some stories in the Bible that are quite shocking to us today and to those that lived through them. Ananias and Sapphira is one.(Acts 5:1) While the church was being formed they lied to the Holy Spirit about an amount of money they had promised to give and dropped dead one after the other. My goodness, it was their money wasn't it? Surely they were free to give what they wanted?

And then, there is the Old Testament story of forty-two boys who are eaten up by two female bears that come out of the woods. (2 Kings 2:24) Who would know that it was because they had talked against a prophet of God. To talk about his baldhead, is that such a crime to warrant the death of forty-two boys. Our idea of what is important and God's idea of what is important is often, not real clear to us mortals.

Chapter 16

WHY, LORD?

The other day I drove through the property known as the 'pair of boots'. The rose bud is now full grown with beautiful two story homes filling up the land that we marched around, claimed for the Lord, blew our trumpet over and anointed the front and back gates. My grandson is still convinced the Lord wants the church, high school and center on that property.

I know this about what we did. We gave it our best shot, we used all our energies and talents, we did not give up when the enemy attacked and we won souls for the Kingdom of God.

What an experience! I know what God meant when He said so clearly to me, "If not you, who?" Everything about me was what the Lord could use. I am truly just a vessel, a ball of clay, useable and moldable. The dream and vision had to be big and it had to be real. I had to believe it. And others had to believe it.

Did we defeat the enemy of gender bias? I don't know. But I know this, when the spirit of gender bias is broken in the church, we will see equality in the pulpit and wholeness in the body of Christ.

When the spirit of gender bias is broken in the church, we will see the abuse of women broken, homosexuality broken, family abuse broken, abortion broken.

When we see sexual discrimination broken in the church, there will be equal pay for equal work, divorce will plummet, husbands and fathers will not abandon their families and there will be respect for one another.

The Counterfeiter is using what he sees in the church and expands it into the world. When we look out on a field and see what kind of fruit is growing, we can know what kind of seed was planted. So, when the seed of gender bias is broken in the church, the world will be affected.

There is no gender bias when the word of Jesus speaks, "You are to go into all the world and preach the Good New to everyone, everywhere . . . and those who believe shall use my authority to cast out demons, and they will be able to place their hands on the sick and heal them." (Mark 16) That call belongs to every believer in Christ Jesus whether male or female, black or white.

There is no gender bias when Jesus tells the women to go tell the disciples of His resurrection and then Jesus had to rebuke the disciples for their unbelief, their stubborn refusal to believe the women's testimony of seeing Jesus alive from the dead. The proclamation of the Gospel message is not subject to the type of vessel He wants to use.

It is my belief that we must work together as team players, partners, servants of the Lord, letting Jesus be the head in order to fulfill the end-time directive of spreading the Gospel.

I personally want to encourage women to get out of the box, whether that box is man-made or self-made, and get into the ministry. It would seem that God will take care of the critics.

When God called me to build a church, high school and center He used certain phrases to get me going. At the time I did not know the significance they held for me personally, and the Christian population. But, I know now.

'Do it now' means that there is an urgency to destroy the enemy that would keep certain folks out of the pulpit and through the drama that our ministry went through, discovered that the enemy could be defeated. But we must take the walk set before us.

'If not now, when?'means the time for women to get involved in the ministry is now. We have a lot of young, vibrant, intelligent, spirit-filled women who are ready to go into the field that is white with harvest and are not satisfied to just be in a holding pattern. This is the season for women to come alongside, roll up their sleeves and get to work.

'If not you, who?' means that God prepared this vessel from the very beginning to go through this task, to feel the pain of rejection in order to find courage to see the enemy face-to-face. He did not call a man for this job. It had to have been a woman.

These phrases that the Lord used on me, I proclaim to you. Get out of the box. You are called to the ministry. Do it now! If not now, when? If not you, who?

CPSIA information can be obtained at www.ICGtesting.com
Printed in the USA
BVOW07s1408170713

326129BV00001B/30/A